Warning!

Before you read this book, you should know that surfing can be dangerous. If you are not careful, and even sometimes if you are, you can break bones, including that hard skull that wraps up your brain. This book explains surfing, but it is not intended to be used as a training manual. If you plan to get on a surf board, protect yourself by taking a few lessons, using the right equipment, always surfing with a buddy, and only doing tricks that you're ready for.

Also, if you do go out and break your head, or any other part of your body or anyone else's body, don't blame National Geographic. We didn't tell you to do it. We told you to be careful!

(Translation into legalese: Neither the publisher nor the author shall be liable for any bodily harm that may be caused or sustained as a result of conducting any of the activities described in this book.)

One of the world's largest nonprofit scientific and educational organizations, the NATIONAL GEOGRAPHIC SOCIETY was founded in 1888 "for the increase and diffusion of geographic knowledge." Fulfilling this mission, the Society educates and inspires millions every day through its magazines, books, television programs, videos, maps and atlases, research grants, the National Geographic Bee, teacher workshops, and innovative classroom materials. The Society is supported through membership dues, charitable gifts, and income from the sale of its educational products. This support is vital to National Geographic's mission to increase global understanding and promote conservation of our planet through exploration, research, and education.

For more information, please call 1-800-NGS LINE (647-5463) or write to the following address:
National Geographic Society
1145 17th Street N.W.
Washington, D.C. 20036-4688 U.S.A.
Visit the Society's Web site at www.nationalgeographic.com.

NATIONAL GEOGRAPHIC

Extreme Sports

SURF!

Your Guide to Longboarding, Shortboarding, Tubing, Aerials, Hanging Ten, and More.

BY SCOTT BASS

Illustrations by Sonia Gauba

NATIONAL GEOGRAPHIC
WASHINGTON, D.C.

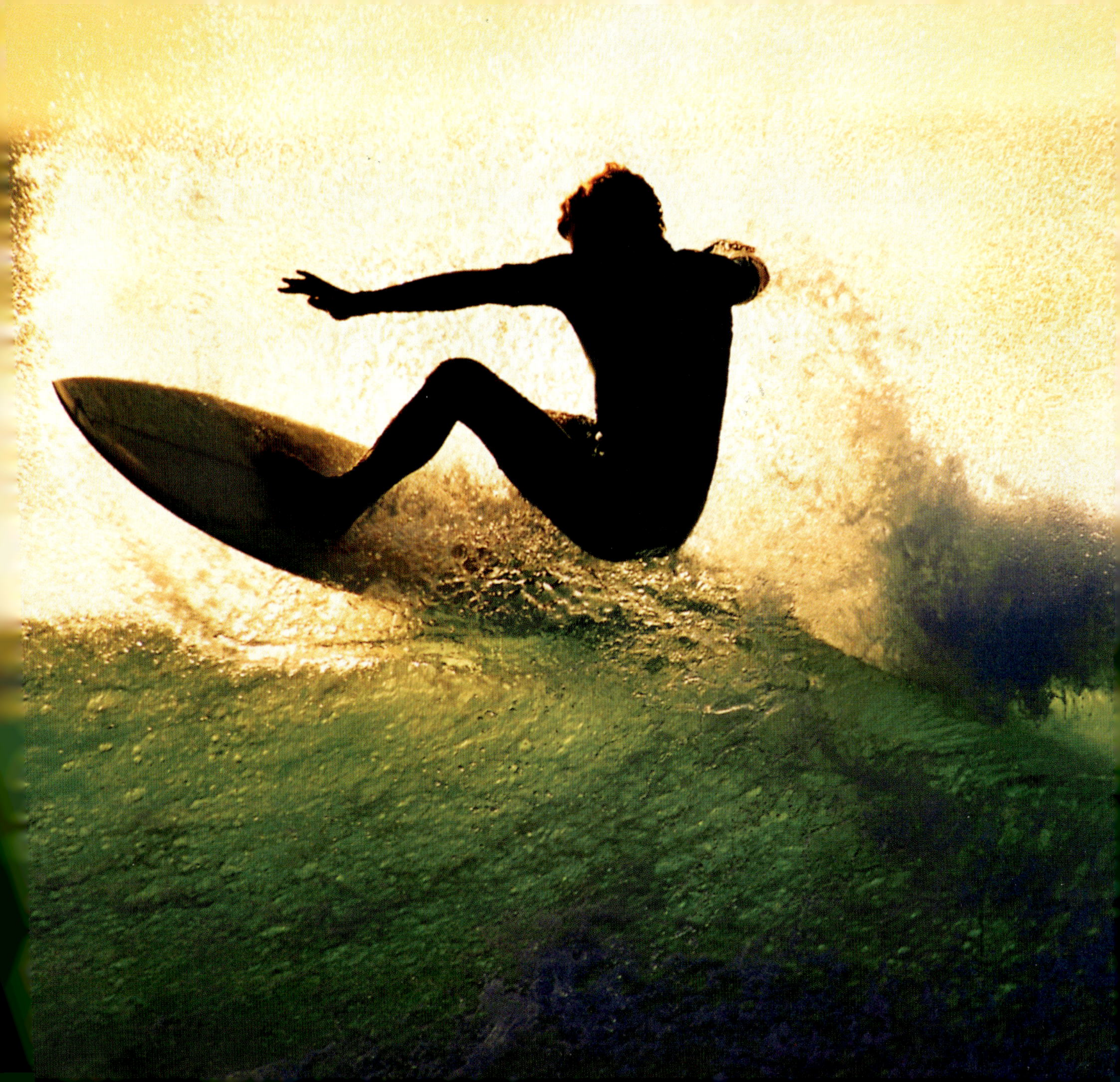

What's Inside

PART ONE: SURFING BASICS
- 10 Getting Psyched to Surf
- 12 Begin at the Beginning
- 14 It's About the Board
- 16 The Long and Short of It
- 18 Getting Ready to Roll
- 20 All Aboard
- 22 Gearing Up

PART TWO: ALL ABOUT WAVES
- 26 It's Simply Science
- 28 A World of Waves
- 30 Master the Monster
- 32 Is Perfect Possible?

PART THREE: TRICKS OF THE TRADE
- 36 Take to the Air
- 38 Hanging Ten
- 40 Tow-In Surfing
- 42 Wild and Wacky
- 44 Artificial Waves

PART FOUR: SURFING THE CIRCUIT
- 48 Competition
- 50 Surfing Big, Surfing Wild
- 52 Hall of Fame: Men
- 54 Hall of Fame: Women
- 56 What It Takes

PART FIVE: PUTTING IT TOGETHER
- 60 Surfing Safe and Sound
- 62 No Waves? No Problem!
- 64 To Find Out More …

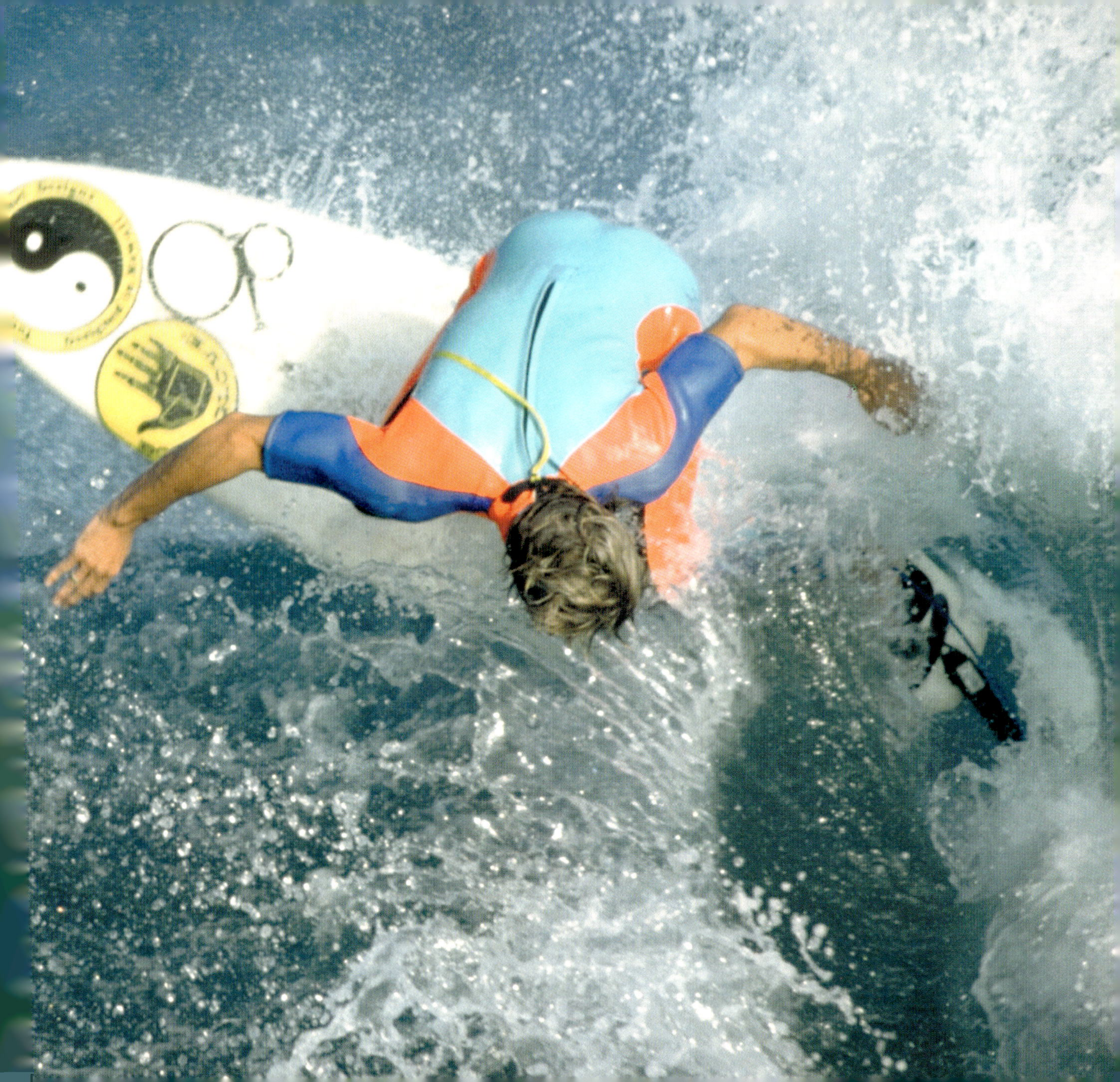

Catch the Wave

Get amped to hit the surf.

Learn the difference between soulful longboarding and radical shortboarding. Get the lowdown on aerials and roundhouses. Power your way through huge barrels at Pipeline with the hottest pro surfers. Learn about amateur and professional surfing competitions. Meet legendary champion Duke Kahanamoku. Understand what it takes to be a world-class surfer.

If you love the beach, the ocean, and the sun, you've picked the perfect sport. But the world of surfing is much more than tropical beaches with warm blue water. Whether it's charging down 100-foot waves, curling 10 toes over-the-nose, or competing in the Dream Tour, this book gives you the lowdown on everything that is surfing.

It's you, your board, and the ocean—so get ready for the ride of your life.

Extreme Sports

Part One

Surfing Basics

- Getting Psyched to Surf
- Begin at the Beginning
- It's About the Board
- The Long and Short of It
- Getting Ready to Roll
- All Aboard
- Gearing Up

You feel the sun on your face. You smell the salt water in the air. Waves are pounding the shoreline. Your board's tucked under your arm and you can't wait. There's your surf break—now, go for it and paddle out!

Getting Psyched to Surf

Jump right in and see what the lure of surfing is all about. It's not just a sport— it's a way to experience nature and water in a whole new way.

Intense. That's the best way to describe riding waves. You feel the energy of the ocean beneath your feet as waves crash all around you. Only a surfer knows the feeling. But riding waves is only the beginning. Surfing is about adopting a new culture, building new friendships, and tapping into nature. It will affect who you hang with, direct the way you spend your time, and guide the personal decisions you make. Surfing is an extreme way of life.

NATURE IN YOUR FACE

Surfing allows you to experience nature up close. From the beach, you can see the ocean, but you can't truly be involved with it till you get out there. And surfing gets you out there into the middle of amazing action. You might see a pod of playful dolphins diving directly below your feet, or feel the slick, oily surface of kelp (a sea plant that grows from the ocean floor) through your fingers as you paddle toward the waves. A thick fog might roll in and chill your bones, or a 20-foot gray whale might blow its spout on you. Each time you hit the surf, a unique experience will present itself.

BREAKING IN

Get ready to search for that perfect wave. As you get into the spirit of surfing, you'll learn all about waves and where the best ones are waiting. Each beach offers a multitude of surf breaks, or spots, to choose from. If the waves at a particular surf break appear too big or powerful, chances are you'll find smaller, more appealing waves at another surf break farther on. As you get more experienced, you can challenge yourself with more difficult breaks.

SINK OR SWIM

The ocean might be fascinating and exciting, but it is also unpredictable. You have no business being there if you can't swim. What looks like a completely harmless wave can rip your board from your arms within seconds. So remember: Never depend on your surfboard for safety. If you want to surf, you must know how to swim—and swim confidently. Before you leave shore, ask yourself if you could swim the distance. If you can't swim out—and back—stay on shore.

TALK THE TALK

Here are some basic terms every surfer should know.

GROM: A young surfer (under age 16; short for grommet, Navy-created slang for "youth").

HEAVY: Difficult, challenging, radical.

PADDLE OUT: To get to the waves by lying on your surfboard, chest down, and propelling yourself through the water as you move your arms in a swift swimming motion.

RIPPING: Making sharp, radical movements up and down the wave face.

SURF BREAK: A particular spot in the ocean, usually near the beach, where the waves form, peak, and explode (also called surf spot).

SESSION: The period of time between entering the water and leaving it.

Groms ▼

Begin at the Beginning

What if you've never surfed before? It sounds like fun, but you want to experience it for yourself. Here are some places to start.

Don't be discouraged when you see a group of professional surfers doing their thing. You can feel that same exhilaration even as a beginner. All it takes is feeling comfortable in the water, being able to swim, and having the patience and determination to learn something new.

CONFIDENCE COUNTS

The ability to swim in a confident and relaxed manner is the first step toward enjoying the ocean. If you feel confident, you will be relaxed. Having a calm, cool temperament in the sometimes scary situations that surfing gets you into is the key to survival. One day, when you're stuck in, say, a vicious rip current the size of Texas, the ability to swim underwater without struggling will serve you well.

SURVEY THE SCENE

The ocean can be a very scary place. Its power is deceiving and often unpredictable. Experienced surfers always take a few minutes to observe the surf before they set out. They look for swell, wave, or wind patterns that help them decipher where the waves are breaking and where the best place is to paddle out. Until you feel comfortable reading the waves, make sure to check in with a lifeguard before surfing. In the summer months, lifeguards often designate areas for surfing and areas for swimming. They'll let you know where it is okay to surf.

TAKE THE PLUNGE

An excellent way to get to know the power of the ocean is to surf it in other ways. For example, try body surfing. Look for breaking waves in the swimming section of the beach, and wait for a good one. Make sure the water is shallow enough so you can touch bottom. You want a wave that is just breaking behind you to get the most of the wave's energy. As it approaches, push off from the bottom with your feet and swim like crazy. You'll know when you've caught the wave—there's nothing like it. You can also try it out with a boogie board, a rubber raft, or even a trash can lid. You will quickly gain an appreciation for how waves roll in, form, and break. Don't be alarmed if you sometimes get rolled by a wave and find yourself with water up your nose—this is all part of the learning process.

TAKE LESSONS

Surf lessons are an absolute must. Every hour you spend with a qualified surf instructor equals 10 hours of frustrating attempts to stand up on your own. Plus, the information you'll attain from a surf lesson is invaluable: Where and how rip currents form; when certain spots in your area break the best; what equipment suits your body size; and where the best deals on equipment can be found. Investigate surf camps. Many offer overnight camping at great surf spots, which can be a lot of fun. You'll get to see yourself surfing on video, enjoy a campfire, and wake up to the sound of the exploding surf.

It's About the Board

Choosing a surfboard is a personal decision. Only you know what kind of surfing you want to do, and the board you choose has to feel right.

Surfboards come in all shapes and sizes. Just as there are many different kinds of waves, there are different kinds of surfboards to ride them. There are also different styles of surfing. You can do high-flying stunts, called aerials, off the waves, or you can take long, leisurely cruises. The kind of surfing you want to do determines which board you choose.

ALL A-QUIVER

Each surfboard design is built with a particular wave type in mind. Because there are so many different types of waves to ride, and different ways in which to ride them, there are a lot of different surfboard designs. Dedicated surfers have a collection of surfboards, called a quiver, to choose from.

SHIP SHAPE

A surfboard's shape, also called the outline, dictates how maneuverable it is on the wave face. Generally, a straighter outline will travel in a straighter line, while a curvy outline will turn up the wave face much more easily. Other features affect what a board can do, including its bottom contour. This shaping on the bottom surface of the board accentuates water flow. It can be flat, concave, double concave, v-shaped, or tri-hull (a design with three places where the water meets the board). Fins are also important: Most boards have at least two fins, but they can have as many as five or as few as one.

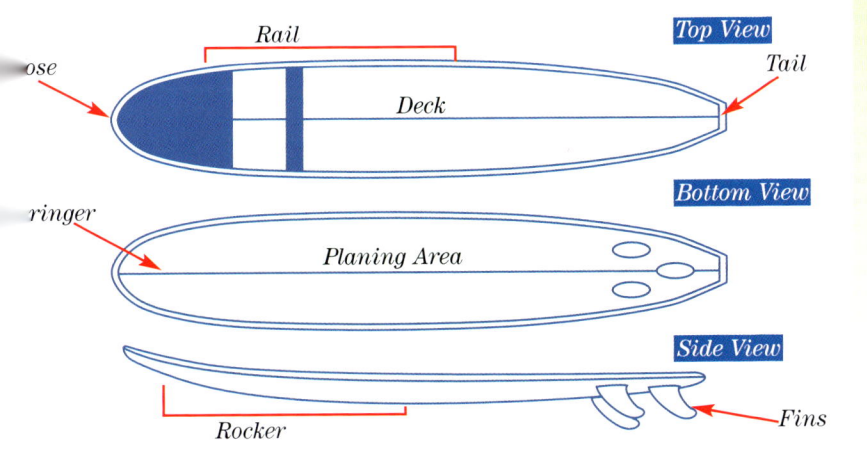

BOARD BASICS

FINS (OR SKEGS): Sharp, angled wedges on the bottom of the surfboard. These provide extra leverage and drive when you lean into a turn. They also supply speed and stability.

NOSE: The first 12 inches of the surfboard. A narrow nose is trickier to balance on, but it enables the board to turn up the wave face quickly. A rounded nose provides more stability and makes paddling easier.

RAIL: The outside edge of the surfboard. Rail design affects the ease of turning while riding a wave.

ROCKER: The bottom curve of a surfboard. A low rocker creates a fast surfboard that won't turn as easily as a high rocker.

STRINGER: A long, narrow strip of wood down the bottom center of a surfboard that provides extra rigidity.

OUTLINE: A surfboard's traceable shape.

TAIL: The end of a surfboard. A narrower tail is good for surfing big waves. A wider tail keeps the board at the bottom of the wave face—making it better for small waves.

FIN BOX: Plastic box to hold the fins in place.

DECK: Between the nose and tail, the portion of the board where you stand up.

PLANING AREA: Where board meets water.

LEASH LOOP: Small nylon cord to attach your leash to (see page 23).

The Long and Short of It

Longboards deliver graceful, leisurely cruises along the waves. Shortboards give you maneuverability, which allows for stunts and high-flying aerials. The choice is yours.

Most surfers have at least one longboard and one shortboard in their quiver. This lets them surf almost all the time, no matter what the conditions. And that's what it's all about—quality time in the water!

PICK YOUR SURFING STYLE

Longboards are great for smaller, less powerful waves. They have more volume and flotation than a shortboard, which makes catching smaller waves a breeze. Longboards are generally at least 9 feet long and have a wide rounded nose. Shortboards are used in faster, bigger waves. Less board means more movement and a faster response to the wave. On a shortboard, you can execute quick, hard turns, aerials, and other stunts off the wave. Shortboards vary in length from 5 to 8 feet, and they usually have a narrow nose area with a multi-finned design.

BLURRING THE LINES

Some dedicated longboarders would argue that if you're good enough, you can do shortboard stunts on a longboard. Others would rather leave the two surfing styles in their separate categories. The traditionalists argue that ripping on a longboard isn't longboard surfing at all. But who says you're locked into one style or another? If you're good enough, and you want to try something different, go for it!

BOARDS FOR BEGINNERS

If you're starting out, bigger is better. A longer, heavier board will give you the stability you need to get comfortable on the waves. Look for one that is taller than you can reach, but also make sure it's not too big for you to carry under your arm. A good starter board is at least 3 inches thick and 22 inches wide in the middle. If you are an advanced skateboarder, skimboarder, or snowboarder, you may be able to start out on a smaller board. But remember: A longer board will always be more stable.

BAG OF TRICKS

Whether surfing on a longboard or a shortboard, you'll want to do more than just stand there. Here's a rundown of the most popular stunts and techniques.

CUTBACK: Turning the board toward the breaking part of the wave, where the most energy is.

GLIDING: Letting the wave's energy carry your board.

NOSERIDING: Curling some of your toes over the nose of your surfboard.

HANGING TEN: Curling all 10 toes over the nose (see page 39).

TRIMMING: Steering the board so that it achieves optimal speed.

WALKING THE BOARD: Using the entire length of a longboard by walking from tail to nose.

OFF THE LIP: Directing the board toward the top portion of the wave and surfing off it. ▼

Getting Ready to Roll

So you're amped and ready to surf. But first you've got to get out there, and in the safest, easiest way you can.

Standing on a surfboard in perfect balance with the wave is the most important part of the surfing experience, but a lot of things have to happen before you can do that. Follow these basic pointers the next time you go out.

STEPPING IN

Always study the ocean conditions for obstacles before paddling out. Recognize rip currents, jetties, piers, and other possible danger zones. There are no umbrella guidelines regarding where to paddle out because each surf spot is different. But as a general rule, obey all posted signs and never paddle out near a pier or rock jetty. Also, note how high the breaking white-water portion of the wave is. Generally, the higher the white-water explosion, the more powerful the surf. Look for gently collapsing white water. Even if it means a longer paddle, you're better off taking the gentler route to get out there.

PADDLING

Position yourself on the surfboard, chest down, so you're properly balanced. If you're too far forward, you will sink the nose underwater and go nowhere. If you're too far back on the board, you'll move, but as slowly as a sea slug. Use swift, strong strokes and always keep your chin up and eyes focused on the horizon. For balance, keep one leg bent at the knee with your foot in the air.

DUCK DIVING

You may have to push through an oncoming wave when you're paddling out. As the wave approaches, paddle hard and then put both hands on the rails of your surfboard. Push the nose of your board underneath the wave while bending your knee and positioning the ball of one foot flat on your board. You want to push that board as far underwater as possible even though your head will probably go underwater too. Wait for the wave to roll past. Then angle the board back toward the surface of the water.

WHEN YOU'RE SURFING...

- Look for advanced surfers and watch them closely. Study what they do and learn from them.
- Stretch out your muscles thoroughly and properly before you paddle out.
- Learning any sport can take a while. Don't get discouraged. Have fun!

WHEN YOU'RE NOT SURFING...

- Go skateboarding or snowboarding.
- Pick up a balance board at your local surf shop and use it whenever you're indoors.
- Watch surf videos and read surf magazines. Study how the pros surf.
- Do pop-ups (see page 21) while watching TV.
- Practice paddling and duck diving with your board in a swimming pool.

Snowboarding

All Aboard

Now you're in the swell, where the fun begins. Get ready for the time of your life.

Surfing is as much about catching a wave as riding one. Perhaps the hardest part of learning to surf is standing, or popping up, once you're in the right spot. After that, it's a matter of balance, motion, and plain old guts.

POPPING UP

Learn to master this critical technique by practicing. Lie facedown on the ground. Position your hands beside your chest and "pop up" onto your feet. Don't touch your knees to the ground. It's one fluid motion. When popping up on your board, you'll push down on the rails. The board will sink into the water a bit giving your knees room to slide underneath your chest. You'll need to figure out if you are "regular" or "goofy." A regular-foot surfer puts the left foot forward. A goofy-foot surfer puts the right foot forward. Use whatever comes naturally as you practice your pop-ups. Your stance should be a little wider than shoulder width with your arms out in front in a relaxed position.

WHITE-WATER RIPPING

If you're a beginner, start out in shallow water with white-water waves. These have already crested and exploded, and they're easy to surf. Position your board facing the shoreline and lie down. Start paddling, and when the wave rolls upon you, hang on. As you zoom off toward the shore, pop up as soon as possible.

CATCHING WAVES

Here comes a wave with your name on it. Paddle over to where you think the crest of the wave will start to topple over, or break. Turn your board around and paddle toward the shore, watching the wave by looking over you shoulder. As you feel the wave start to rise underneath, you'll feel your board moving faster. This means you've caught the wave. Now's the time: Pop up, throw your feet underneath your chest, maintain a wide, stable stance, and push your weight forward on your front foot.

THE ART OF THE WIPEOUT

Wipeouts are an everyday occurrence. No surfer is immune to the stinging ego bruise of wiping out in front of friends. But there is an art to wiping out, and it's important to position yourself so you don't get injured. First, always cover your head with your arms to protect your head from your surfboard. Second, try to enter the water almost parallel with the ocean surface. You'll be less likely to hit the bottom if you're in a shallow area. Third, when you come up to the surface, keep your arms over your head, again to protect yourself from your board.

Gearing Up

The waves are rough and the water may be cold. Make sure you're outfitted properly before you start paddling out.

In some ways, going surfing is simple. There are no admission fees, no lift tickets, and no tests to take. All you need is your surfboard, a little wax, and some waves. But once you get seriously interested in the sport, you'll also need some gear.

WETSUIT

This standard surfer's outfit will keep you warm, allowing you to stay in the water longer. Made primarily of neoprene, a synthetic rubber that's especially tough and insulating, a wetsuit should fit snugly. It works by letting in a thin layer of water and using your own body heat to keep you warm.

You might also want a rashguard, a shirt made of Lycra, to protect your skin from chafing against your wetsuit. And if you're paddling out without a wetsuit, the rashguard will protect your skin from the wax on your board. You should also wear booties to protect your feet from rocks and shells.

LEASH

This tough plastic cord attaches to the ankle of your rear foot and connects to the tail end of the surfboard. You need it to keep your surfboard nearby when you wipe out. It's also an essential safety device to make sure your board doesn't shoot toward other surfers or swimmers.

BOARD EXTRAS

The noseguard is a soft plastic tip that fits onto the nose of your board. Not only does it protect your board, but it protects you too. A surfboard's nose can be sharp. Tailguards are another option. And for extra sure-footedness when going for aerials and other high performance moves, outfit your surfboard's tail with deck traction pads. If your board has a fin box, you can remove the fins to sample other fin shapes and designs.

Serena Brooke waxes her board. ▶

GOOD WAXATION = NO FRUSTRATION

Surfing wax is sticky. You need it on the deck of your surfboard to keep your feet from slipping. Here are few tips to make sure you get a dependable wax job.

- Strip off any old wax with de-waxing products such as combs and solvents.
- Work in a cool, dry area, such as your garage.
- Apply a coat of base wax using long lengthwise strokes from nose to tail. Base wax is very hard and forms small bumps on the board's deck. Use one full bar of base coat per 5 feet of board. When the wax is worn slick, you can use a wax comb to rough it up or take it off. If the wax is too hard to strip off, leave the board in the sun for five minutes before stripping the wax off.
- Next, apply a generous wax topcoat (warm, cool, or cold water wax, depending on the water temperature where you are surfing).
- Re-apply a thin layer of topcoat before every session. Now you're done. No slipping means better ripping!

Extreme Sports

Part Two

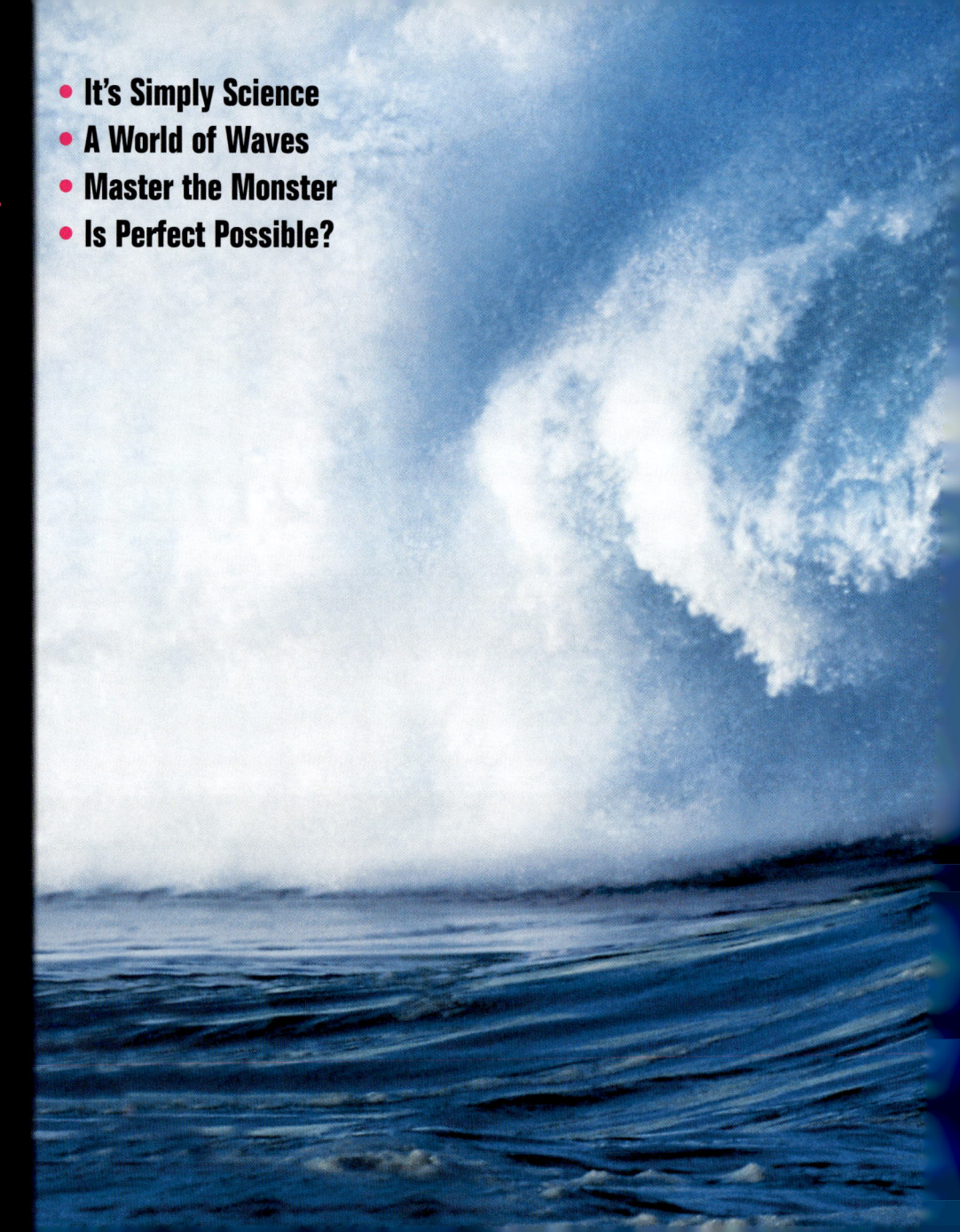

All About Waves

- It's Simply Science
- A World of Waves
- Master the Monster
- Is Perfect Possible?

When you're surfing, the ocean is your playing field—or obstacle course. You can work on your own skills, but you have no control over what kinds of waves nature is going to serve up. The best approach? Learn how to surf them all.

It's Simply Science

Waves are dynamic. That may be the reason surfing is such a rush—unlike a skate ramp or a ski slope, this sport's surface is moving energy.

Though earthquakes and the gravitational pull of the moon have small parts in wave formation, ocean wave energy is primarily created by wind. Wind creates ripples. Over time, the ripples pile on top of each other and form waves. These waves eventually ride upon each other and form swells. Ocean wave energy travels thousands of miles as ocean swells. These swells finally disperse their energy when they explode at a surf break.

BREAK DANCING

As waves enter shallow water, they move closer together. They also slow down and grow taller. Eventually, a wave's top will spill over and it becomes a breaker. Waves break differently depending on what's under them. A wave will break with a "tube" when it arrives abruptly at a shallow bottom. A tube is a hollow, barrel-shaped tunnel. It's every expert surfer's dream. A wall-like wave breaks all at once because the ocean floor is unbroken by a reef or deep water trench. Wall waves are hard to surf because they don't offer much wave face for riding on. Areas with varying depths produce peaky waves that are angled and break in a nice, linear fashion. Points, jetties, piers, and reefs often create changes in ocean floor depth and help make good surfing waves.

DEGREES OF EXCELLENCE

Another factor in shaping waves is the direction from which the waves approach. If waves come into a beach straight on, they may get walled up. Local storms can break up the wave direction, or offshore islands can "shadow" the swells blocking them from reaching shorelines. A slight angle to the swell direction creates an ideal wave form for surfing.

POCKET OF ENERGY

Ride as close to the breaking wave as possible, positioning and turning your board tight within the open wave face. This is the pocket where the energy is. You must speed up or slow down to stay in the pocket. To gain speed, bury your inside rail in the pocket. Lean slightly down and forward with your weight on the inside rail.

PARTS OF A WAVE

TUBE: The hollow tunnel created by the breaking crest of a wave. Also known as the barrel, shack, green room, pit, and lumpy wagon.

CREST: The top of the wave when it has reached its peak and is ready to fold over

GREEN WAVE: The area of a wave, before it breaks, where the energy has accumulated.

LIP: The curl at the edge of a breaking wave's crest.

POCKET: In a breaking wave, the area that holds the most energy.

TROUGH: The bottom of the wave or the low point between two waves.

WHITE WATER: The broken section of the wave where energy is dispersed.

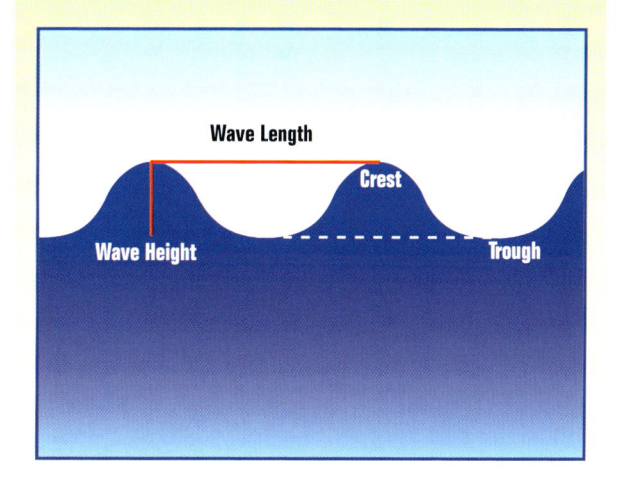

A World of Waves

Like the surfers who ride them, no two waves are alike. Each has its own size, shape, and personality. Some waves are neat, soft, and playful. Others are windswept, lumpy, and downright violent.

No matter what, when a wave reaches the shallow water of a surf break, you can't tell what it's going to do. A seemingly playful swell can roll onto a shallow reef and turn into a mean and ugly wave in a hurry. Just down the beach, that same swell can roll through a soft sand bar, break slowly, and lap upon the beach almost unnoticed.

A powerful 20-foot beach break wave

WAVES FOR EVERY LEVEL

The type of waves you choose to ride depends on your ability. Learn as much as you can about the waves at your beach. Talk to people at the surf shops about the best surf breaks for someone of your ability.

PEAK PERFORMANCE

A-FRAME: A peaked wave with an open, unbroken green wave face on each side of the crest. Generally ideal for surfing.

PEAKS: Lots of A-frames rolling into the beach.

WINDSWELL: A wave condition generated by wind. Short interval, consistent surf. Sometimes choppy, but usually peaky.

GROUNDSWELL: A wave condition generated by powerful storms hundreds of miles away.

WALLS: Long waves that fold over and explode in one motion. Generally not good for surfing.

POINT WAVES: Waves that break across, or perpendicular to, a headland or small peninsula. These usually break over large stones or boulders. Point waves are ideal for surfing because they offer lots of open wave face to ride on.

BEACH BREAK WAVES: Fast, powerful waves that break on a sandy bottom. Sometimes these become walls.

REEF WAVES: Strong, powerful waves that form over rock or coral reefs. They usually stand up out of deep water.

MUSHY WAVES: Waves that break softly and with little power. These are good for beginners.

HOLLOW WAVES: Powerful tunnel-shaped waves for experts only.

TSUNAMI: A dangerous and extremely powerful wave usually caused by an oceanic earthquake (also called "tidal wave," even though it has nothing to do with the tide).

TOP FIVE

While all surfing beaches can have powerful waves on any given day, these five spots enjoy a global reputation as having the most powerful waves on the planet. Although Australian beaches didn't make the list, powerful surf lines much of the country, especially on the east coast. Top big wave sites in Australia include Bondi Beach in the east and Kirra Point on the Gold Coast (shown below).

JAWS: A picturesque reef break on the Hawaiian island of Maui.

WAIMEA BAY: Famous big wave spot on Oahu.

BANZAI PIPELINE: Notorious hollow wave on Oahu, with big tubes.

MAVERICK'S: California's cold-water version of Waimea Bay.

TEAHUPOO: Ridiculously thick, or wide, wave scene on the main island of Tahiti.

Ideal ruler-edged point waves ▼

Master the Monster

Just how much wave are you willing to chew off? Just remember to match the surfing technique with the wave because every wave has its own surprises.

It doesn't matter if the wave is 1 foot or 100 feet tall—the idea is to stay close to the energy. How? By staying in the pocket of the wave. But certain waves are gentle while others can be downright harmful. One wave will give you cool, cruising bliss, while another is nothing but a fight. So adjust your attitude accordingly.

RAIL-TO-RAIL

When surfing the type of point waves found at Malibu Beach, California, you can have fun by turning your board up and down the wave. It's all about transferring your weight from one rail to the other using a heel to toe motion. Angle your board's inside rail into the wave face by putting weight on the balls of your feet. You will pick up speed as the board rises up the wave. To drop back down into the trough of the wave, rock back on your heels to shift weight to your outside rail. This will steer the board downward. As you reach the bottom of the wave, apply pressure to the inside rail by shifting weight to the balls of your feet. Called rail-to-rail surfing, it's the same technique used to turn a snowboard or a skateboard.

Now you're ready to gouge a turn into the wave face. Look down the line for the spot where you'll be making your move, and aim your board there by shifting your weight to the inside rail. As you get ready, put all your weight on the outside rail of your board. Let the speed carry your outside rail through the turn. Keep your hands on the board to guide it in the direction of your turn.

SURFING THE ROUGH STUFF

As you gain confidence and venture out into larger surf, forget about pulling off cutbacks and other turns. Instead, focus on completing the ride successfully without wiping out. This is rough surf, and you must respect it. As the wave approaches and you start paddling towards it, summon your confidence. Brace yourself for some bumps in the road. Absorb these bumps by widening your stance. Aim for a point somewhere in the channel and lean into your bottom turn by applying pressure to the inside rail.

Always be thinking of an escape route in case the wave throws an awkward bump or tube your way. One escape is to simply dive off your board and swim deep. Wait for the wave to roll over you, and then scramble for the surface. Get on your board and get back out before another wave rolls through. Another good method of escape is to straighten off your ride and angle your board toward the shoreline. Then lie down on your board and ride out the explosion.

MALIBU: LONGBOARD HEAVEN

Surfrider Beach in Malibu, California, is formed by a large river mouth. It's got three distinct points, or surf breaks: First point is the farthest inside point, second point is the next one, and third point is the farthest out. First point is considered the ultimate longboard wave. When you hear people say they surfed Malibu (shown below), they probably mean first point.

Is Perfect Possible?

How dedicated a surfer are you—really? Would you go to the ends of the Earth just to find the perfect wave?

Someone once said, "A perfect wave is one that puts a smile across your face." To a surfer, that would mean almost all waves are perfect. But philosophy aside, a perfect wave is the ultimate canvas on which to paint your surfing masterpiece. A perfect wave offers you the opportunity to ride the inside tube, execute a series of maneuvers, and go extremely fast. Here are a few surf spots which, with the right tide, swell, and wind conditions, produce what many consider perfect surf. But if you can't get there right away, you can always dream.

Surfing Jeffrey's Bay, South Africa

RINCON, CALIFORNIA: The Queen of the Coast. Here, you'll find ruler-straight, long point waves that break along a stony bottom. Swells come in from storms raging hundreds of miles away and arrive in a steady stream.

JEFFREY'S BAY, SOUTH AFRICA: Another ruler-edged, long point wave scene. The scenery is beautiful, as Jeffery's Bay is part of the eastern Cape and bounded by mountains. Rides here can go for as long as a quarter of a mile.

G-LAND, INDONESIA: A beautiful, lush tropical backdrop frames this intense lefthander. Here, the wave breaks go left (usually, when facing a beach and paddling into a wave, you have the choice of going right or left). The waves at G-Land are long and fast, but also hollower than waves found at most favored surfing destinations.

SUNSET BEACH, HAWAII: A deep-water reef break on Oahu, which produces some of the most intense rides anywhere. Rides aren't as long as what you'll find in the other places, but pound for pound, they are just as exhilarating.

THE ENDLESS SEARCH

In the 1960s, filmmaker Bruce Brown set off on a surf adventure with two young surfers, Mike Hynson and Robert August. Their journey took them around the globe exploring various surf spots and capturing their adventures on film. One day, on a beach in South Africa, Hynson glimpsed a wave peeling off in the far distance. As the other two lay asleep, Hynson walked along the beach toward the waves he'd noticed from afar. When he got there, Hynson's jaw dropped in disbelief. Perfect waves rolled in, one after another, as if a machine was pumping them out. Hynson had stumbled upon Cape St. Francis. Brown filmed as August and Hynson surfed the perfect waves all day long. The result was the climactic sequence to the most famous surf movie ever made, *The Endless Summer*.

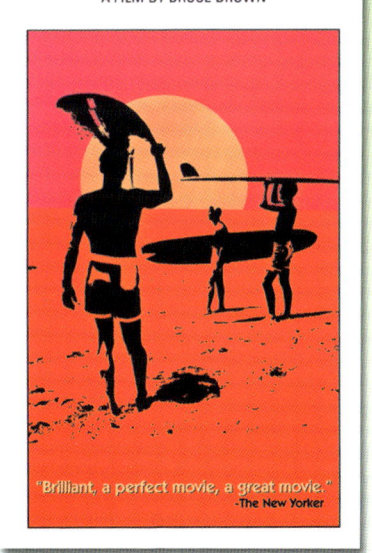

The movie was an instant classic playing to sold-out audiences across the United States even in the dead of winter. Eventually, it made more than $8 million in profits (and Brown's initial investment was only $50,000!). The movie's re-release on video and DVD in 2000 made it available to a whole new generation. Today, thanks to the influence of *The Endless Summer*, traveling is very much a part of the surfing lifestyle. Dedicated surfers travel to exotic beaches all over the globe hoping to turn a corner, or peer down from a sand dune, and stumble upon the type of wave perfection discovered by Mike Hynson.

Extreme Sports

Part Three

Tricks of the Trade

- **Take to the Air**
- **Hanging Ten**
- **Tow-In Surfing**
- **Wild and Wacky**
- **Artificial Waves**

Riding waves on a board is a magical experience. But if you're into extreme sports and you want to go the distance, you'll want to do more on your surfboard than just stand there looking cool. Catch the latest in radical stunts, or finesse a perfect hang ten.

Take to the Air

In any extreme sport, going airborne is the name of the game. Surfing is no exception. The way to take it to a new level is to take it up.

The surfing aerial is a move that came from skateboarding and snowboarding. So, you are way ahead if you can skateboard or snowboard—better yet, if you can perform aerials on either board. But to execute aerials and other stunts on a breaking wave, you also have to know what you're doing as a surfer.

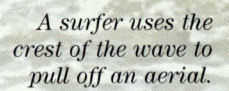

A surfer uses the crest of the wave to pull off an aerial.

WAVE SELECTION

Waves that are too flat won't offer enough speed or a proper launching section. What you want is a steep, vertical wave to give you plenty of down-the-line speed and offer great launching sections. If you're not going fast, you won't have a chance. So build speed by pumping your board from rail to rail.

PREPARE FOR LIFTOFF

Fix your eyes on a launching area—usually a cresting section somewhere down the line of the wave. As you approach, stay high in the pocket and close to the lip. Do not go down to the bottom of the wave. Stay high and stay committed to the move.

MIND THE GAP

When you get to the launching zone, de-weight. This means removing the leg pressure you've been applying to gain and maintain speed. You must hit the launch section and then relax the leg pressure as you fly through the air. Think about allowing a gap between the deck of your board and your feet. Timing is crucial. If you de-weight too soon, you won't get in the air.

TAKE YOUR PICK

Before your launch, work out what type of aerial you want to pull off. Go with what's comfortable. If you want to grab your board in midair, choose one of the following: front hand grab (reaching for your board in front), backhand grab (reaching behind you), no hands, or stalefish air (reaching behind yourself to grab the tip of your back leg's heel). Whichever one you choose, it's a good idea to keep your leash on.

AERIAL MANTRA

Here's a great "paddle thought" to play through your mind as you prepare to boost big airs in the surf.

SPEED

COMMIT

DE-WEIGHT

RELAX

Recite these four words over and over in your mind to get psyched.

A surfer wipes out on an aerial move.

Hanging Ten

Get ready for the ultimate stunt in longboard surfing. Are you psyched to walk the plank?

While aerials are the hottest, most advanced move for shortboard surfing, hanging ten is the most advanced maneuver for longboard surfing. Lots of surfers can hang five toes over the nose. But to balance perfectly with all 10 toes curled over the nose is quite an achievement. Like all maneuvers in surfing, hanging ten requires balance, timing, and great wave judgment. Oh yeah, style is important too!

Hanging five: one step away from a hang ten.

STALLING OUT

You'll need time to set up the nose ride, so it's important to choose a long, lined-up wave, one that isn't too steep. Start by dropping into the flats of the wave and leaning into a long, drawn-out bottom turn. This will bring you up the wave face slowly, allowing for the board to stall out. You want to slow the board's speed as it rises up the wave face.

WALKING THE PLANK

With the board rising up the wave face, almost at a complete standstill, the "set up" portion is complete. Now you'll have to get that log moving again, and this is where the noseride comes in. Walk up to the nose using a cross-step technique (moving straight forward on the board will create drive or momentum). Shuffling toward the nose is not acceptable. You must walk, one foot crossing over the other, until you've reached the front portion of the nose in order to keep momentum. This movement is almost a dance step, similar to an Irish jig.

THE MOMENT IS NOW

Now that you're at the nose, place your front foot lightly on the tip of the surfboard making sure to drape five toes over the nose. Your rear leg is planted firmly behind you and carrying all your weight. Once you're comfortable, quickly slide your back leg up to meet your front leg and drape the other five toes over the nose. Don't look now, but you're hanging ten. It's not too late to flash a smile and throw your arms over your head in majestic surf pose. Congrats—you're practically walking on water! Keeping your balance and maintaining speed may require you to adjust by sliding your back leg quickly behind you.

Cross-stepping in action

WORK IT

Practice cross-stepping using a sidewalk curb as a makeshift balance beam. Get into your surfing stance and begin cross-stepping by lifting one foot over the other foot. Continue this all the way down the curb. Remember—no shuffling.

Tow-In Surfing

What do you do when the good surf is simply too far out to paddle to? If you want to surf it anyway, find someone with a personal watercraft.

Tow-in surfing is a relatively new and radically extreme version of surfing. Usually, two surfers team up and take turns towing one another to where the big waves are. One drives a high-powered personal watercraft (PWC) and tows the other surfer on a board. Read about it here, but don't try it—tow-in surfing is for adults only!

HOW IT'S DONE

As a large set of waves approaches, the driver positions the PWC towards the waves as the other surfer, already in a stand-up position, gets ready. When the time is right, the driver guns the PWC at full speed and whips the surfer into the wave. The surfer lets go of the towrope and immediately rides the wave at top speed. This style of surfing is only for the most advanced surfers. These aquatic daredevils ride gargantuan waves with some swells reaching 70 feet. Tow-in surfers put themselves in life or death situations each time they motor out to the lineup.

THE TOW-IN RUMBLE

Although tow-in surfing is generally respected, some traditionalists say that if you can't paddle into the wave on your own power, you shouldn't be surfing. They argue that big wave surfing requires perfect wave judgment, timing, and strength—all of which are compromised by the machinery involved with tow-in surfing. Some go so far as to describe it as glorified water skiing. Others argue that the spiritual nature of the sport is lost when you add machinery to the mix.

TOW-IN GEAR

PWC: Runs at about 160 horsepower with a top speed of 70 MPH. In most states, you need to be old enough to drive before you can get a license to operate one.

TOW-IN BOARDS: Tow boards must be able to withstand the punishment, so they are made with multiple layers of fiberglass. The narrower outline, foot straps, and heavy construction of the tow boards set them apart from conventional surfboards.

SLED: Almost 6 feet long, made from polyethylene foam with vinyl-tubing hand loops on each side, the sled attaches to the back of the PWC. It is the lifeline between the driver and the surfer during an emergency rescue.

PFD: A personal flotation device assures that if a surfer or driver gets into trouble, eventually he or she will float up to the surface.

ROPE: A standard water ski rope made from braided marine-ply nylon with a foam-padded flotation handle.

Tow-in Board

PWC

Sled

Wild and Wacky

Surfing's no different from any other extreme sport. People are constantly looking for ways to push the envelope: What's the highest wave ever surfed, what are the riskiest stunts ever performed? Fasten your wetsuits everybody…

When it comes to extremes, surfing has them in spades. On the one hand, there's the raw power of nature producing waves as tall as a six-story building. On the other hand, there's the surfing mentality. No stunt is unthinkable or impossible for the brave of heart. But be warned: Some are dangerous.

Working toward a perfect Rodeo Clown Flip

FINDING THE GIANT WAVES

On a clear Friday morning in February of 2001, Mike Parsons' life changed forever. The night before, Parsons and a crew of big wave tow-in experts had chartered a boat for the Cortez Bank, a low ridge of underwater mountains 10 hours off the southern California coast. Within a few hours of arriving at Cortez Bank, Parsons' tow partner, Brad Gerlach, revved their PWC toward a huge ocean swell. With split-second accuracy, Gerlach gunned the PWC and whipped Parsons into a gargantuan 60-foot wave. Some say it was the largest wave ever ridden. Still, a few other surfers could probably challenge that claim, like big wave surfer Ken Bradshaw of Hawaii. Somehow, someway, someone will probably break the record. As technology makes swell prediction programs more reliable, PWCs more powerful, and tow-board design more refined, the general consensus within the surfing community is that someone will eventually ride a 100-foot wave.

RODEO CLOWNS

The popularity of aerial surfing is at an all-time high, and the capacity for coming up with wild new stunts knows no limits. One of the craziest aerial moves is the Rodeo Clown Flip. While in the air, the surfer grabs the surfboard with both hands and does a complete back flip before landing back on the wave. The only Rodeo Clown Flip to be executed successfully was documented in 2000. The surfer was red-hot Floridian ripper Aaron Cormican, and the aerial was shot on video. Nevertheless, rumors abound that local kids are pulling off the remarkable Rodeo Clown Flip up and down the seaboards of both coasts.

A FIVE-MILE RIDE

The ocean isn't the only place where people surf. The River Severn in England is one of just a few rivers in the world with surfable waves. When the river water pours out and the ocean tide moves in, a natural wave phenomenon, known as a bore, creates a surge wave (so called because of the sudden rise in water level). A surge wave can be surfed, using a very long board. Other rideable bores occur on the Amazon River, at the Cook Inlet in Alaska, as well as rivers in China and India. Bore waves roll upstream for miles making for unusually long rides. The current world bore surfing record is a ride of 5.7 miles.

A surfer rides a surge wave in Cook Inlet, Alaska.

Artificial Waves

The trouble with good surfing is that it depends on nature to deliver the goods. But what if we could create perfect waves on our own?

With the supply of first-class waves limited by the realities of nature, it was only a matter of time before someone dreamed up the notion of artificial waves. One way to make them was to build artificial reefs in the ocean, which would create waves out of arriving swells. Another idea was to build wave machines in enormous water tanks.

A surfer tries to keep his balance in an artificial surfing environment called a Flowrider.

PRATTE'S REEF

In 1984, a pier built to influence the tide was constructed near El Segundo, California. Unfortunately, it ruined the surf. So the Surfrider Foundation (an environmental group dedicated to preserving surf spots) teamed up with Chevron, U.S.A., and the California Coastal Commission to build the first artificial surfing reef in the United States. The reef is named after Tom Pratte, the Surfrider Foundation's first executive director.

Pratte's Reef is made of sandbags weighing 14 tons each. The bags are arranged in a wedge formation, which is perfect for creating good surfing waves. The designers chose sandbags so that if the experiment went wrong, the reef could be destroyed without causing major damage to the environment. Pratte's Reef has an estimated life span of about 10 years. So far, the reef has failed to produce good, surf-friendly waves. But, the ocean floor is constantly changing, so no one is ready to write off Pratte's Reef for good. Only time will tell.

SURFING IN A BOWL

The Flowrider is a large, fiberglass, pool-like structure that uses specially designed pumps to thrust water toward a padded wall. When the water rushes over the Flowrider wall, it flows into a perfectly formed tubular wave. It looks and acts like an ocean wave, but its riding characteristics allow you to perform skateboard and snowboard tricks as well as standard surfing. The Flowrider has received critical acclaim from professional extreme sport icons such as Tony Hawk, Terje Haakonsen, and Christian Fletcher and is the centerpiece of a major professional tour.

WHERE TO FLOW-RIDE

There are more than 20 Flowriders located around the world. Here are the locations of those in North America.

San Diego, California

Redlands, California

Vista, California

Kissimmee, Florida

New Braunels, Texas

Dallas, Texas

South Padre, Texas

Hyland Hills, Colorado

Lake Lanier, Georgia

Great Falls, Montana

Cincinnati, Ohio

Two surfers try out Flowrider waves.

Extreme Sports

Part Four

Surfing the Circuit

- **Competition**
- **Surfing Big, Surfing Wild**
- **Hall of Fame: Men**
- **Hall of Fame: Women**
- **What It Takes**

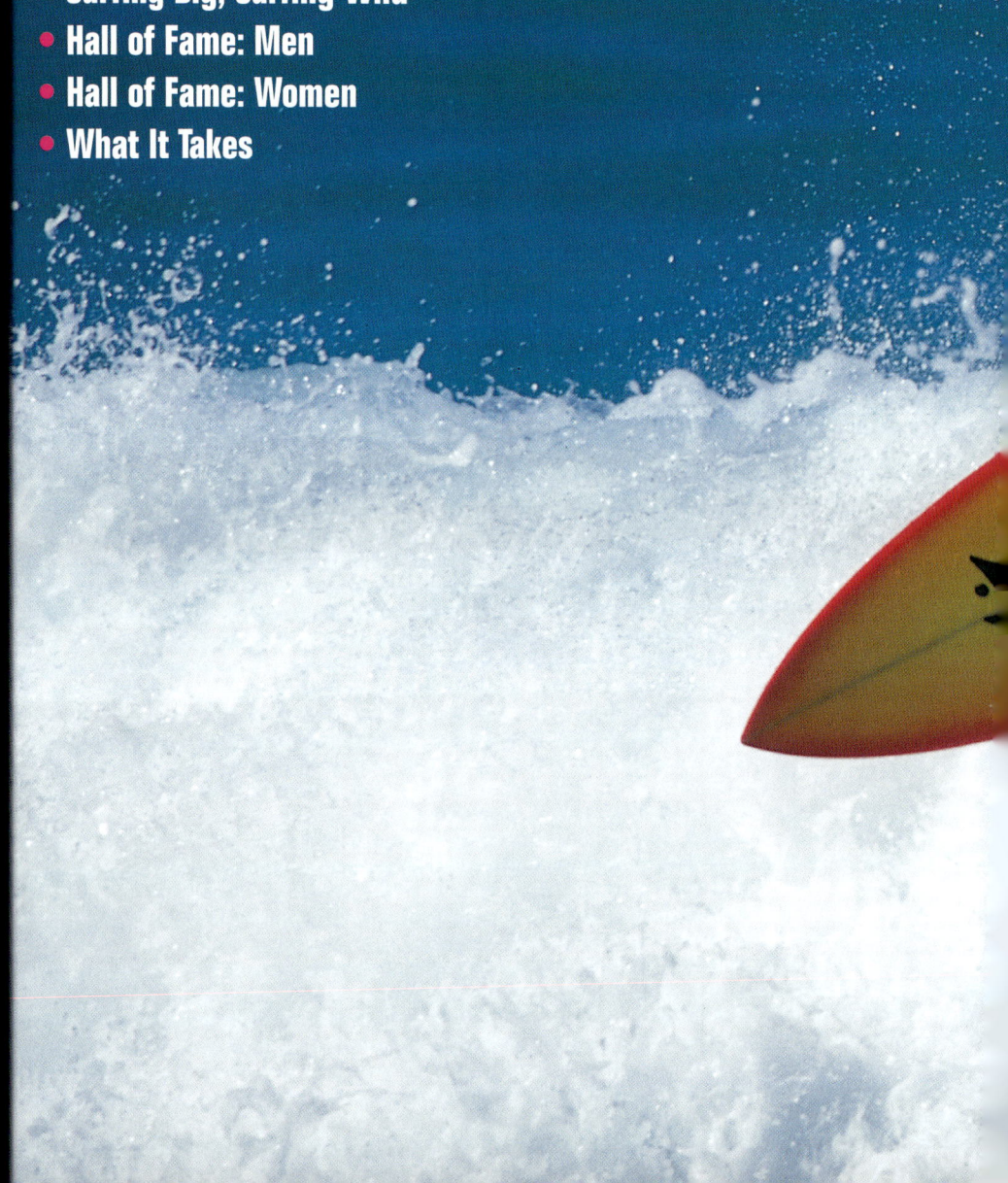

Face it—surfing is all about performance. You're performing for yourself, but chances are, other people are watching you from the beach. Now take it up a notch and see what it takes to be a champion.

Competition

Most surfers dream of becoming great. But what does it take to be the best?

To become the world's greatest surfer, you have to be born with talent. You must nurture that talent through training, surfing experience, and just plain guts. And you must be 100 percent dedicated to your goal. You can work on your ultimate goal by aiming for smaller goals along the way. There is a whole range of surfing competitions out there to give the truly dedicated, competitive surfer a chance to shine. Start early in life and you'll have a jump on the competition.

Competitor Sunny Garcia at the 1999 U.S. Open of Surfing, Huntington Beach, California.

LOCAL BEGINNINGS

The two primary amateur surfing organizations in the United States are the National Scholastic Surfing Association (NSSA) and the United States Surfing Federation (USSF). These organizations offer local contests for practically every young surfer with competitive ambitions. In the surf culture, the NSSA and the USSF are roughly the same as Little League or Pop Warner, and this is the place to develop your competitive surfing skills. If you're good enough, you'll be invited to surf in the national competition that crowns a U.S. amateur champion every year.

THE PRO-AM LEVEL

The next competitive step you take toward your goal is the pro-am, or "professional-amateur." It is in this arena that you will meet up with other top-notch amateur stars. And they're not just from North America. The hottest young surfers from all over the world meet to do battle and gain recognition from the surf industry. Many of them begin international rivalries with surfers who they will compete with for the rest of their professional surfing careers. In the United States, the Professional Surfing Tour of America (PSTA) and the Foster's Pro Tour are just two of many pro-am circuits.

THE DREAM TOUR

After surfing successfully at the amateur level and competing vigorously on the local pro-am circuit, the next step is the World Tour of Association of Surfing Professionals (ASP). The ASP World Tour begins with the World Qualifying Series (WQS), a series of events that determines which pro surfers qualify for the World Championship Tour (WCT). The WCT events are held at famous surf spots around the globe. If you qualify for the WCT, you'll be surfing the famous Pipeline in Hawaii, Tahiti's treacherous Teahupoo reef, and the perfect point waves at Jeffrey's Bay in South Africa. The waves can get so good during the WCT events that the surfers call the contest the "Dream Tour."

A crowd of surfers at the Pipeline in Hawaii surveys the competition.

Surfing Big, Surfing Wild

They're fierce, they're huge, and they mean business. Big waves—waves 20 feet and taller—offer the ultimate rush when it comes to the competitive arena.

With mainstream interest in big wave surfing at an all-time high, thanks in part to the incredible feats of tow-in surfers such as Laird Hamilton and paddle-in pioneers such as Flea, it was inevitable that big wave surfing would enter the competitive scene. Today, there are three standout big-wave events.

TOW-IN WORLD CUP

The annual Pe'ahi Tow-in World Cup Championship is the world's only tow-in, big-wave contest. In January 2002, the inaugural contest took place in spectacular surf off Maui, Hawaii. Each team consists of two competitors, one PWC driver and one surfer, who switch roles as part of the competition. The championship is held at different times every year. Organizers block out a period of time from mid-November to mid-January and wait for the big waves to come in on the Maui site. The championship kicks off as soon as judges say the waves are big enough, which means at least 40 feet high.

QUIKSILVER

Quiksilver, a surf apparel and lifestyle company, holds two separate paddle-in big wave events. The first one honors one of Hawaii's all-time greatest big wave surfers, Eddie Aikau, who died in 1978 in a powerful storm. Held at Waimea Bay, the organizers of Quiksilver Eddie Aikau keep a close eye on the winter swells that regularly pound the North Shore of Oahu. Once the waves get large enough, the organizers quickly notify the list of big wave invitees that the event is on.

The Quiksilver Men Who Ride Mountains event is held at Maverick's, the notoriously mean and wide wave scene at Half Moon Bay, just south of San Francisco. This contest is also an "invite only" event, and like its Hawaiian counterpart, organizers set aside a few months every year and wait for the biggest swell before giving it a green light. Waves don't always cooperate, and when they don't, the events are postponed to maintain the integrity of the competition.

TOP GUN AIR SHOWS

Aerials weren't a big part of competitive surfing until recently. Although most surf contests awarded points for performing maneuvers on a wave, competitors didn't want to risk radical maneuvers such as aerials and lose points if they wiped out. Now, thanks to air shows, or surf contests that are based solely on aerial surfing, competitors can perform all kinds of radical stunts without worrying about being overly penalized for falling.

A Quiksilver competition poster

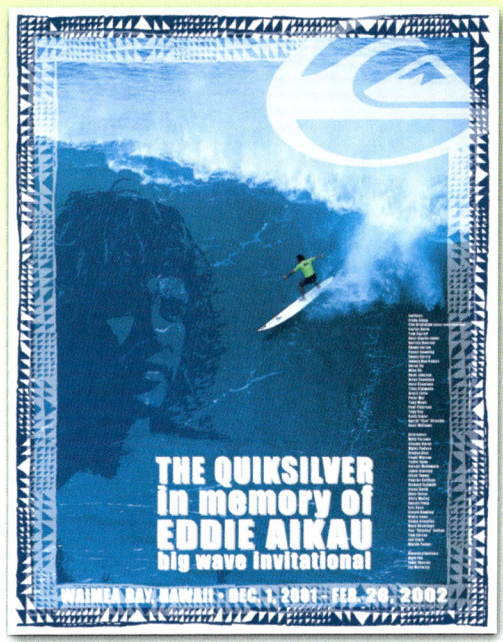

Hall of Fame: Men

From the father of modern surfing to today's boy wonder, these male champions have helped shape and define the art of competitive surfing.

It was once a man's world—surfing, that is. Early surfing legends were fearless men blazing a trail. Newer pros, such as Kelly Slater and Taylor Knox (shown here), keep up the tradition.

DUKE KAHANAMOKU

Duke Paoa Kahanamoku was an Olympic gold medalist swimmer, actor, and the official patriarch and ambassador of modern surfing. Born in 1890, Duke grew up in Waikiki and, like most Hawaiian boys, became an expert swimmer, lifeguard, and surfer. At age 22, Duke qualified to swim in the 1912 Olympic Games in Stockholm, Sweden. On his way to the games, he stopped in California and gave a surfing demonstration in Corona Del Mar, officially spreading the surfing craze to the mainland. Two years later, he went to Australia and demonstrated his surfing ability for almost three hours. News of his thrilling exhibition quickly spread through Australia, and soon surfboards were popping up on all the beaches near Sydney.

Duke Kahanamoku standing with surfboard, Hawaii, circa 1910.

KELLY SLATER

Slater's the Michael Jordan of professional surfing. With six ASP World Championships, Slater is generally considered the greatest surfer ever. He's also a world-famous celebrity having appeared on the cover of Interview magazine, acted in the "Baywatch" television series, and produced a music CD and several surf movies. Slater grew up in Florida. He began racking up competitive success at the amateur level, and by age 15, he was well on the way to surfing greatness. Like Jordan, Slater has an incredibly competitive nature and hates to lose.

THE IRONS BROTHERS

Andy and Bruce Irons hail from Kauai and are two of the world's hottest surfers today. Innovative moves, full-rail speed surfing, and deep tube positioning characterize the Irons brothers' superb technique. Throughout their careers, the brothers—only two years apart in age—have spurred each other on with rivalry and inspiration.

TAYLOR KNOX

Born in Carlsbad, California, in 1971, Knox had a rough start, undergoing back surgery at age 15 because of a skateboarding injury. But only months after his recovery, Knox was ready for action, placing well in the NSSA Open Season and joining the national team. Knox sealed his place in surfing history by becoming the first surfer ever to win $50,000 on one wave. This happened at K2 Big Wave challenge in 1998 when Knox rode a 52-foot wave.

Hall of Fame: Women

Surfing may have started out as a man's game, but it didn't stay that way.

Women began entering the competitive circuit in the 60s and 70s. Since then, a number of female superstars have emerged, including Layne Beachley (shown here).

MARGO GODFREY OBERG

A true pioneer in the arena of women's surfing, Oberg got her start in La Jolla, California. As a teenager in the 1960s, she had no problem impressing guy surfers with her abilities, winning the Western Surfing Association amateur title at age 15—just four years after learning to surf. She won a World Championship title later that same year.

LAYNE BEACHLEY

A native of Sydney, Australia, Beachley has won three World Championships so far. In 1998, she won five out of 11 WCT events and clinched the crown for that year. Her well-rounded approach serves her well in both small and medium-sized waves. But Beachley is held in highest regard for her big-wave surfing ability. She is one of the few women to tow-in surf in the large and unruly outer reef waves off the Hawaiian Islands.

SERENA BROOKE

Born in Australia in 1976, Brooke first hit the amateur circuit in Australia in 1990, at the age of 16. Soon after, she clinched the Queensland and Australian national titles. As a professional, she rose quickly through the ranks and became the ninth best female surfer in the world in 1997. That year, she attained stardom with an outstanding performance at the Quiksilver Roxy Pro at Sunset Beach, Hawaii. "I just want to keep winning and set a good example because I think the girls are starting younger and getting a lot more support than in years past," says Brooke. "There are girls out there learning and they need role models." *(see Serena on p. 23)*

BIRTH OF A HOLLYWOOD LEGEND

In 1955, 16-year-old Kathy Kohner spent her entire summer at Malibu. The zany cast of surfers—including Tubesteak and Moondoggie—who frequented Malibu took Kathy under their wing and nicknamed her Gidget. "I'm so small, they called me midget," explained Kathy to her father. "I got so mad that now they call me Gidget. A girl midget." Her father wrote a best-selling book about his daughter's fun-filled summer adventures at Malibu. The book soon became a series of popular movies about a young surfer girl, which helped give surfing national exposure. Eventually, the movies spun off into a television series with Sally Field in the role of Gidget. Today, surfing is more popular than ever with females. Girls are signing up for surf camps in California in record numbers, and the most money spent on a surfer movie to date went to "Blue Crush," a film about young women surfers that was released in August 2002.

What It Takes

Learning to be the best requires relentless dedication and training. But the fun part is, you get to surf as much as you possibly can.

To join the ranks of Kelly Slater (right), with his six ASP World Championships, it helps to be gifted with natural talent and physical strength. You must learn to surf at a young age and practice constantly. But most important of all is that competitive fire that marks a true winner.

PHYSICAL PERFECTION

Professional surfers are required to twist their bodies in all sorts of strange positions. This is why a strong, flexible, and loose body is ideal for surfing. You don't want to build up too much muscle mass, or you will lose flexibility. But it's important to have strong legs and glutes so you can power your board through the water and take it to the best part of the breaking wave.

YOU CALL THIS WORKING OUT?

There are a number of different ways in which professional surfers stay in top physical condition. Not surprisingly, professional surfers surf all the time, and this is by far the best way to stay in shape for the sport. Because it is so much fun, pros often spend up to six hours a day "working out." When the waves are small or conditions in the ocean aren't favorable, many top pros stay in shape by swimming. In fact, swimming is a great way to get exercise whether you want to be a star surfer or not. Water creates a natural resistance that is enough to tone and shape muscles without adding unwanted stress on your body. Twenty to 30 minutes of stretching, before and after exercise, is the other crucial training element that professional surfers have adopted. Many top pros even go through a yoga routine before hitting the water. The yoga stretches and postures help surfers keep their bodies strong, yet relaxed and flexible, and loose enough to be ready for anything they might encounter in the water.

DEEP-SEA DIVING

Big wave surfers train a little differently from the average pro surfer. After all, they rarely get a chance to practice in the big stuff. One workout uses large rocks on the ocean floor. The surfers dive down to the bottom, pick up the rocks, race each other along the ocean floor, dump the rocks at the finish line, and swim back up to the surface. This regimen helps surfers build up lung capacity, helps them cope with different depths and stressful conditions, and trains them to stay calm in life-threatening situations.

Extreme Sports

Part Five

Putting It Together

- Surfing Safe and Sound
- No Waves? No Problem!
- To Find Out More ...

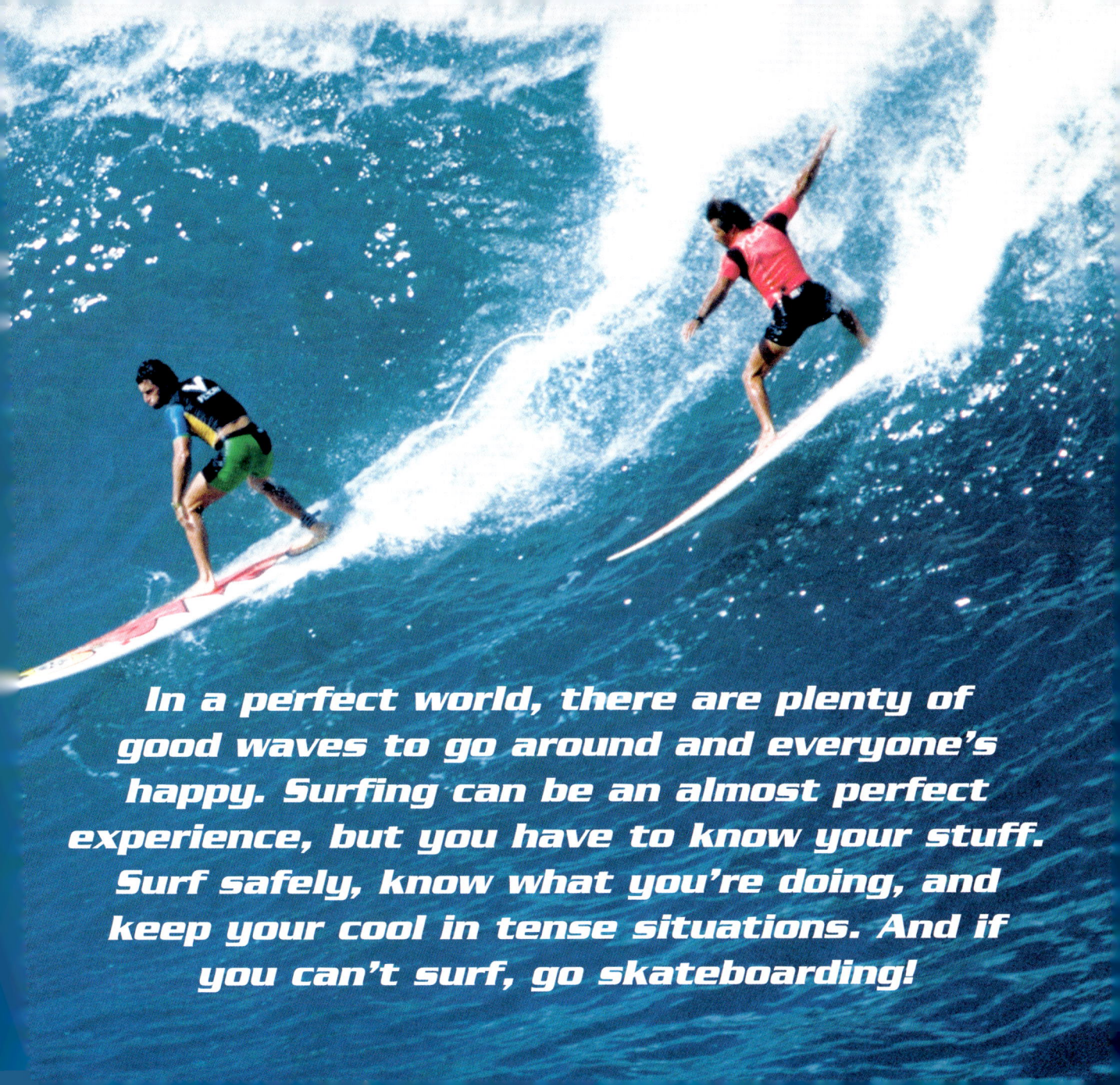

In a perfect world, there are plenty of good waves to go around and everyone's happy. Surfing can be an almost perfect experience, but you have to know your stuff. Surf safely, know what you're doing, and keep your cool in tense situations. And if you can't surf, go skateboarding!

Surfing Safe and Sound

Part of surfing's excitement is the danger. But never forget to surf responsibly and within your limits.

Here's a useful bit of wisdom: "The best way to get respect is to give respect." This is especially true when surfing. Always respect the ocean, the elements around you, any wildlife you encounter, and other surfers in the water. And the best way to respect your fellow surfers—and your own safety—is to follow a few basic rules.

RIGHT OF WAY

- If you're learning to surf, pick a beach that isn't crowded with other surfers.
- When paddling through the surf, never throw your board aside. Also make sure your leash is secure.
- If two surfers are attempting to catch the same wave, the surfer closest to the pocket, or breaking wave, has priority. If in doubt, pull out and wait for the next wave.
- Never surf alone. Instead, go with a buddy. One of you might need the other's help in case of an emergency.
- Before paddling out, study the conditions. Don't go if you don't feel comfortable with the situation.
- If a wave is coming to you, and you recently had a good ride, offer the wave to the surfer next to you. Usually when you give a wave away, there will be another one right behind it with your name on it. Give a wave, get a wave. It's good karma.

TERRITORIALISM VS. LOCALISM

Some surfers think if they live near a particular beach, they have more rights to the waves at that beach than other surfers who don't live nearby. Territorial surfers will often use foul and abusive language to scare people off. Ignore them. We live in a free society, and the ocean belongs to everyone.

Surfing locals go to a particular surf spot on a regular basis. They can be a good source of information, so don't be afraid to ask them questions: Where's the best place to paddle in? Are there any strange currents or reefs to worry about? What's the best board for the spot? You'll learn a lot from them.

SURF RAGE

Unfortunately, there is an ugly side to the surfing culture. Often, surf spots will be so crowded that tempers flare. Sometimes the conflict is just a battle of words, but other times it can get physical. The most important thing you can do in this type of situation is keep your cool. Paddle away to avoid trouble. If a fight breaks out, go tell a lifeguard or police officer. But keep in mind that 99 percent of all surfers are non-violent. Generally people go surfing to relax and have fun, not to fight.

Crowded conditions sometimes result in a fight for surfing territory.

No Waves? No Problem

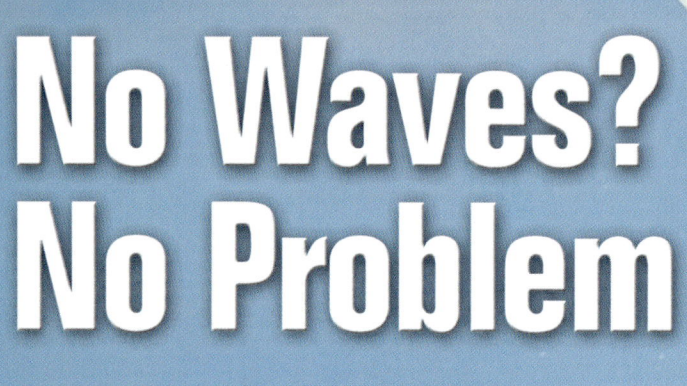

Not everyone's lucky enough to live next to awesome surf year-round. What do you do when you've just got to surf but there's nowhere to go?

There are any number of ways to tap into the exhilaration of surfing without catching waves. Several other sports, such as wakeboarding (shown here), use the same moves and basic principles as surfing.

JUST GO BOARDING

Skateboarding, snowboarding, wakeboarding: All these board sports have a lot in common with surfing. They require the same muscle action, coordination, and balance, and they're (almost) as much fun. To become a better surfer, spend as much of your down time as possible participating in these sports when you can't get in the water for a surf. Skateboarding is by far the best of the board sports for practicing balance and turning. Best of all, you don't need a motorboat or a ski slope to do it.

TRY THIS AT HOME

Consider investing in a balance board to keep in shape and work out at home. These boards let you practice the balancing skills you'll need to be a good surfer. The best balance boards let you practice the various balance positions required for surfing.

WATCH IT ON TV

Watching high action (and highly entertaining) surf videos should be a staple of your schedule. Check out Taylor Steele's *Momentum* while you're eating breakfast. Or watch *The Endless Summer* with some friends next Saturday night. You can't lose by watching the world's best surfers pull into huge frothing waves and take to the air. It's a thrilling way to improve your own surfing skills.

THE SKATEBOARD CONNECTION

Skateboarding was born in the 1950s due to the increasing popularity of surfing. A group of California surfers, wanting to express their surf style on the street, added some roller-skate wheels to the bottom of several two-by-fours, and suddenly, a new sport was born. Surfers rode their "skateboards" down perfectly sloped hills, leaning into bottom turns and streaking through imaginary tubes. Over the years, skateboarding swept the nation, and sidewalks from Malibu to Massachusetts were swamped with excited young "sidewalk surfers" terrorizing the pathways. Today, the skate/surf connection has gone full circle as the top surfers attempt to perfect the radical aerial moves developed by their extreme sport counterparts, the skaterboarders.

To Find Out More...

ADDITIONAL INFORMATION

WEBSITES

Ezines
www.surfermag.com
www.transworldsurf.com
www.surfline.com

Surfing camps
http://www.club-ed.com
http://www.paskowitz.com/surfcamps.html
http://www.surfsdsa.com/surfcamp.htm
http://www.kahunabob.com

BOOKS

Bustin' Down the Door by Wayne Bartholomew (Harper Sports, 1996)

Longboarder's Start-Up by Doug Werner (Tracks Publishing, 1996)

Surfer's Start-Up, Second Edition by Doug Werner (Tracks Publishing, 1999)

VIDEOS AND DVDS

The Endless Summer (Image Entertainment, 1966)

The Endless Summer Revisited (Monterey Home Video, 2000)

Momentum (Image Entertainment, 1992)

Transworld Surf Hit & Run (Redline Entertainment, 2000)

ORGANIZATIONS AND ASSOCIATIONS

National Scholastic Surfing Association
PO Box 495 Huntington Beach, CA 92648
(714) 536-0445   www.nssa.org

International Surfing Association
5580 La Jolla Blvd; PMB 145
La Jolla, CA 92037
(858) 551-5292
www.isasurf.org

Association of Surfing Professionals
PO Box 309
Huntington Beach, CA 92648
(714) 848-8851
www.surfingamerica.org

Surfrider Foundation USA
P.O. Box 6010
San Clemente, CA 92674-6010
(949) 492-8170
www.surfrider.org

ABOUT THE AUTHOR

Scott Bass grew up surfing in Del Mar, California. He earned a B.A. in Literature and Writing with an emphasis in writing from Cal State San Marcos. He has surfed extensively in California and Mexico as well as Indonesia, Fiji, Tahiti, Central America, Europe, Australia, and the Caribbean. He is currently the Online Editor at SURFER Magazine and is also a contributing photographer and features writer for the magazine.

PHOTO CREDITS

Cover: Vince Catatio/Getty Images

Corbis: Pages 2-3, 6, 7, 8-9, 12, 20, 22, 24-25, 28, 30, 34-35, 61, 62; Corel: Pages 4-5, 10, 14, (wave)16, 17, 21, 26, 32, 36, 37, 39, 42, 50, 58-59, 60; QuikSilver: Pages 11, 51; PhotoDisc: Pages 13, 19, 57, 63; Kahanamoku Sons: Page (surfboards) 16; Tom Servais: Pages 18, 23, 31, 46-47, 49, 52, 54, 56; Bruce Brown Films: Page 33; Pierre Tostee/Getty Images: Page 38; Donald Miralle/Getty Images: Page 40; Steve Kornreich/Hydrofoilsurfing.com: Page 41; Ron Niebrugge/wildnatureimages.com: Page 43; Water Mania: Page 44; Paramount Kings Island: Page 45; Jeff Gross/Getty Images: Page 48; Bishop Museum: Page 53; Universal Pictures: Page 55

Copyright © 2003 National Geographic Society

All rights reserved. Reproduction of the whole or any part of the contents without written permission from the National Geographic Society is strictly prohibited.

Library of Congress Cataloging-in-Publication Data

Bass, Scott.

Surf!: your guide to longboarding, shortboarding, tubing, aerials, hanging ten, and more / by Scott Bass.

p. cm. – (Extreme sports)

Summary: Provides instruction in everything from getting used to being in the ocean to surfing in professional competitions.

ISBN 0-7922-5108-3 (pbk.)

1. Surfing – Juvenile literature. [1. Surfing. 2. Extreme sports.] I. Title. II. Series: Extreme sports (Washington, D.C.)

GV840.S8B37 2003   797.3'2—dc21   2002012761

Design: Todd Cooper, Sonia Gauba, designlabnyc
Editorial: J. A. Ball Associates
Series Design: Joy Masoff